CONTENTS

SECTION 1 — *INTRODUCTION*
Have you got what it takes to become self-employed?; how this Pack can help you 2

SECTION 2 — *GETTING STARTED*
Developing your current line of work or buying a business off the shelf?; franchises; the lead-up to going it alone; sole trader/partnership/limited company? 4

SECTION 3 — *IS THE BUSINESS VIABLE?*
The business plan; profit and loss forecast; cash flow forecast; financing the business 8

SECTION 4 — *RUNNING THE BUSINESS*
All the admin. side: business name; bank accounts; deciding your terms of trade; putting yourself on the map; premises; insurance; computers; patents, service and trade marks and registered designs; your pension 13

SECTION 5 — *VAT*
How it works; who needs to register; simplified schemes 19

SECTION 6 — *ACCOUNTS AND INCOME TAX*
Keeping accounts; all about income tax (including your accounting year; allowable business expenses, capital allowances); National Insurance 22

SECTION 7 — *EMPLOYING PEOPLE*
Recruiting staff; equal opportunities; contract of employment (paying employees, maternity rights, sick pay, pensions); problems with employees; employees' National Insurance and PAYE 28

SECTION

1 INTRODUCTION

Every year, hundreds of thousands of people decide to take the plunge of working for themselves. Not all of them succeed. Many end up realising that they just had not known what they were letting themselves in for. Others who are better prepared may still not find it all as they had expected, particularly as ups and downs in the economy affect their businesses. But for thousands of others, working for themselves is the start of a new life in which they can use their skills and experience to start up successful enterprises.

Financial rewards there may be, but running a profitable business also brings other benefits. No longer at the beck and call of a superior, you can devote yourself to serving your client or customer. Your fate is in your hands: only your enthusiasm and drive can ensure business success. This can be a thrilling prospect, but it can also challenge you deeply: you may need to develop new skills (to deal with book-keeping, for example) and be prepared to extend yourself to the farthest limits of your abilities. You will need all the help you can get.

HOW THIS PACK CAN HELP YOU

Plenty of help is available to you as a budding entrepreneur if you know where to look for it. Some of this is free, some is available at low cost because of support from the taxpayer, some you will have to pay the full rate for. Knowing the right questions to ask, whom to turn to and how to use the answers is essential in finding your way through the challenge of working for yourself – and this Action Pack is designed to help you do just that.

The Pack offers a brief guide to the main questions you need to think about when launching a business. These questions are summarised for handy reference on the checklist in the back pocket of the Pack. There are copies of two worksheets to help you plan your business, one to make sure that it will be profitable and the other that you will have enough cash to see it through. And there are details of sources of information and advice in the back pocket, with a list of useful addresses and telephone numbers.

No guide to self-employment can cover every aspect of starting your own business: each enterprise is different and some information will be highly specific to your line of work. This Pack offers general guidance to people starting a business full-time, whether on their own, in partnership or as a limited company. If you are setting up a partnership or limited company, you will certainly need further guidance, and even the simplest of small businesses will benefit from professional advice. The services of a sympathetic accountant are indispensable; you will probably need legal advice; and a supportive bank manager will greatly ease the task. Friends who are already in business should be able to give you recommendations, or see if the sources of advice listed on page 6 can help. Ask for some indication of the cost of any advice you need, which will normally depend on the amount of time involved and (perhaps) the complexity of the work.

There are plenty of longer books dealing in more depth with the issues raised in this Pack, including some on detailed aspects such as accounting methods. There are also specialised works on particular lines of business such as retailing, exporting, building etc. Expect to supplement this Pack with a visit to a good bookshop or a local library to find the detailed information you need.

Two Consumers' Association books which you might find helpful are:

- *Starting your own business*, which expands much of what is touched on in this Pack, with some useful worked examples
- *Earning money at home*, designed specifically for people looking to work from home, part-time or full-time.

Other useful CA publications are mentioned where appropriate, and are available through bookshops, including the *Which?* shop at 359–361 Euston Road, London NW1 3AL, or from Consumers' Association, PO Box 44, Hertford SG14 1SH.

HAVE YOU GOT WHAT IT TAKES?

Section 2 looks at the sort of planning you need to do to get your business started. But it takes more than just a good idea or talent to succeed in business: you must have what it takes to work for yourself, to see through the project in good times and bad. Try to answer the following questions about your motivation and commitment before taking the plunge:

- *why do you want to work for yourself? Is it really what you want to do?* If you are just fed up with your present job, or thinking about self-employment until a job turns up, think again. You need positive motivation to succeed, and a half-hearted approach could be disastrous
- *are you prepared for the lack of security?* If you work for someone else, you are used to job security, regular pay, set hours and holiday, fringe benefits, pensions etc. Working for yourself means providing all these things for yourself – and no work means no pay
- *can you cope with working on your own?* Going to work imposes a routine, providing companionship from colleagues and direction from your superiors. You will have to impose your own work pattern and discipline, and get used to working by yourself. Even if you employ others, the buck will stop with you
- *how will you cope with adversity – even failure?* Most businesses go through a bad patch sooner or later, and it needs determination to see them through. Remember that you may have to get into some considerable debt to finance your business, so failure can mean bankruptcy
- *are your family prepared for the change?* Their moral support will be essential, especially if things get hard, yet they may see less of you and have to put up with less income for a while.

One way to test yourself on these questions is to start off in your spare time, if this is possible. Although this is not the same as taking the plunge, at least you can get a feel for the challenges and how the job would work out.

SECTION

GETTING STARTED

You may already know exactly what line of work you want to take up, particularly if it involves developing the sort of work you are already in or turning a hobby into a business. This section looks at some organisational preparations which will help make a success of your business.

▬ DEVELOPING YOUR CURRENT WORK

Many people setting up in business do so to continue freelance the work they have been doing for their employer or as a spare-time job. This avoids the need to learn a new trade, and means that you will have established contacts with potential customers, suppliers and other people you might need to work with.

Going it alone with your current line of work is not all plain sailing:

- you will have to deal with all sorts of problems which were sorted out by your former employer without your involvement. These include arranging supplies, marketing, delivery, dealing with customers and chasing payments
- customers you currently deal with may not want to move their business to you. They may stick with your former employer who has supplied them reliably for many years and who may be able to offer better terms than you can (longer to pay, for example)
- you may even find that you are not allowed to set up in competition with your ex-employer for a while, under a clause in your contract of employment.

Developing a spare-time business into a full-time one also needs preparation to make sure that there is sufficient work. Can you increase your customer base enough to make up for the loss of earnings from employment? You will have to adopt new ways of getting work, running your finances and handling the work. Change is rapid in business and you cannot expect to continue working in the same way for very long: you will have to develop it as the years go by, finding new products and customers.

▬ BUYING A BUSINESS OFF THE SHELF

Buying an existing business can overcome some of the problems of starting up on your own: it will have established customers and suppliers; there will be some sort of product or service with a reputation (not necessarily a good one); and records for the organisation and its finances should already exist. There may also be stock of raw materials or goods, fixtures and fittings, premises, patents or franchise agreements and other assets.

On the other hand, a business is usually sold for good reason:

- it may be making a loss, with customers melting away, goodwill exhausted, suppliers owed money and the books in a mess. Why is the business making a loss and how you can make it perform differently?
- it may be so profitable that the owner wants to cash in on his or her hard work. The price will reflect this success, and you might find it hard to improve the performance further.

If you're buying an existing business, ask your accountant to look at its operation and go through the books *before* you part with your money. And since the biggest asset of many small businesses is the goodwill of the existing customers and suppliers, ask a solicitor for advice on steps to preserve that goodwill (for example, by ensuring that the previous owner doesn't set up in competition down the road). Check that important aspects

4

of the goodwill can be transferred (the business name, say, or franchise agreements).

There are extra checks to make if the business you're buying involves premises. The lease should be examined by a solicitor and searches made of the local authority to see whether there are planning restrictions or other proposals in the pipeline which might affect you.

FRANCHISES

A company which has developed a successful business idea may expand its activities by licensing other people to use the same idea locally as their own businesses, by franchising. For someone going into business, buying a franchise offers many advantages, including (usually) a successful product or service and a system of running the business which is tried and tested, backed up by the company selling the franchise. Another benefit could be that of being associated with a well-known product, which is nationally advertised. And if the franchise is set up properly, you may be able to enjoy a trading profit virtually from the start, rather than having to work for months or years to establish yourself.

Because of these advantages, the franchise is unlikely to come cheap. Just buying the right to a good and profitable franchise can cost tens of thousands of pounds before you start trading. You will have less freedom to develop the business as you please (the franchise agreement may specify things like the decor of your premises and where you must buy supplies). There may be restrictions on whom you can sell the business to, which could reduce your return on retirement or selling up early. And the company selling the franchise will know from experience just how much it can rake off in commission (10 per cent of turnover – not profit – is about average).

Beware of cowboy franchisors: their start-up fees may appear attractively low, but they tend to offer little or no back-up or cream off all your profit. Franchisors who belong to the British Franchise Association are bound by a code of ethics which offers some protection to franchisees. And a reputable franchisor will be happy to put you in touch with other franchisees to discuss their experiences. Discuss any franchise you are considering with professional advisers: a solicitor to scrutinise the agreement and an accountant to examine the business plan (the high-street banks have specialist departments which can do both for you).

PREPARATIONS

Whatever your chosen business, use the time leading up to its launch to prepare for going it alone. Try it out in your spare time, at the weekend or during your holidays. Even if this confirms your decision, you will pick up useful information and experience. It may also reveal the need for more preparation.

Research

Find out as much as possible about your product or service and the market for it:

- talk to others in the same business, especially people you won't be competing with (a trade association might be able to put you in touch)
- find out about your competitors and what you can offer that they can't. Send off for their promotional literature and price lists and have a look at their premises
- once you have fixed a price or fee, try it out on potential customers – firm or even tentative orders will help in raising any finance
- research the market. Larger county and city libraries and specialist business libraries will have census reports, market research, company annual reports and the business press.

The Small Firms Service of the Department of Employment produces a series of useful guides on matters such as marketing, exporting and selling to large firms. These should be available through your local Training and Enterprise Council (TEC).

Advice

There are plenty of organisations and individuals that can offer advice to new businesses on general matters such as your business plan and finances, but also on detailed matters relating to the type of product you have in mind. They can often draw on the experience of people who've been successful in business, and offer support after you have got going. Among organisations to consider are:

- local enterprise agencies (contact these via Business in the Community) and chambers of commerce
- local Training and Enterprise Councils (TECs)
- the small business advisers in most high-street banks
- the Rural Development Commission
- the specialist development agencies in Scotland, Wales, Northern Ireland and some English regions
- Project FullEmploy if you're from an ethnic minority
- The Prince's Youth Business Trust
- industry and trade associations and research establishments such as PERA (the Production Engineering Research Establishment).

In some cases, you will be directed towards commercial consultants. The Department of Trade and Industry Enterprise Initiative will contribute towards the cost of such consultancy (within limits), including that for marketing, design, business planning and information systems. Telephone Freefone Enterprise for more details.

A solicitor's advice could be worth taking, especially if you need premises, intend using a patent or adopting a trademark, or need to offer guarantees or indemnities.

Training

If working for yourself involves a new line of business, ensure that you have the necessary training (even if you get it by working part-time in the field). Also consider training in other aspects, including marketing, computing and financial management. Being able to touch-type could turn out to be at least as valuable an accomplishment as holding City & Guilds in your subject.

Evening classes may be available in many basic business skills, or you could consider correspondence courses. Some of the bodies listed above for advice also run training sessions, with opportunities to test out ideas before taking the plunge. If you're prepared to take on more advanced studies, you can follow various Open University courses right up to MBA, or take short courses at local university and polytechnic business schools.

There is also a considerable range of vocational and business training courses lasting from one week to sixteen weeks run by the Employment Service and local Training and Enterprise Councils (TECs). There's normally a fee to pay unless you are unemployed (though you may be able to get tax relief on it). Many courses are full-time, but you may be able to take part before becoming self-employed by using your holiday or taking unpaid leave.

HOW TO ORGANISE YOUR BUSINESS

One important decision to make is the legal status to adopt for your business: sole trader, partnership or limited company. There are other less common options, including co-operatives and unlimited companies. The decision is important because it will affect how your business is organised, financed and taxed.

The most important choice to be made is between being a company with limited liability and remaining unincorporated as an individual sole trader or in partnership with others. Discuss this decision with your business advisers at an early stage.

Sole trader

A sole trader is completely and solely responsible for the business: you take all the profits, but you are also responsible for the losses. If you can't pay debts the business incurs, you are personally liable and can be made bankrupt, losing your home, savings and personal possessions.

Although many people think a business has to be a company, it is often better to start off as a sole trader. It is the most flexible form of business organisation with little red tape involved in setting it up. You don't have to deduct tax or National Insurance from money you draw from the business (though you do have to pay these in other ways – see Section 6). And you can set losses off against other types of income, even getting a rebate from the Inland Revenue (see page 27).

Enterprise allowance

If you have been unemployed for eight weeks or more, you may qualify for a state benefit to help you launch your own business. Enterprise allowance pays you £40 a week for up to a year, provided you can find £1,000 to put into the business. For more details, contact your local Training and Enterprise Council (TEC).

Partnership

Two or more people (up to a maximum of 20) can form a partnership to run a business as a single legal entity. Some partners can be 'sleeping partners', putting in cash (and drawing profits) but not actively working in the partnership. Each partner is liable for the debts of the partnership, so if one doesn't pay, the other partners must cough up. And as for a sole trader, liability is unlimited: you can be made bankrupt to pay the partnership's debts.

Although partnerships are common in professions such as law and accountancy, choosing the right partner(s) is essential. Partnerships that go sour can be messy and upsetting and end lifelong friendships. A partnership agreement should be drawn up by a solicitor setting out what each partner puts in and gets out (i.e. the share of the profits), how the money will be held (e.g. who signs the cheques), whether salaries will be drawn, how decisions are taken, how the partnership will be ended.

The partnership is taxed as a single person, and the tax bill is divided between the partners (if one partner doesn't pay, the others are liable). Losses are also divided between the partners and each can use them in much the same as a sole trader. Partners pay the same National Insurance contributions as sole traders.

Limited company

A company is a legal entity in its own right, distinct from the people who work for it or own it. It can continue to exist after you stop working for it and you can pass it on to your children or sell it to a complete stranger. If you set up a company, you would be a director and a shareholder. If you pay yourself any salary, income tax and National Insurance must be deducted under PAYE from it; if the company pays you a dividend, advance corporation tax is due on it.

The main advantage of a company is the option of limited liability: by choosing it, the shareholders who own the company are liable to lose only the money they put into the company in buying shares. If a limited company goes bust, the shareholders can't be made to pay the debts (though the directors might if they were trading while insolvent). In practice, the benefits of limited liability may be less than at first appears: banks and others who lend money to small companies often demand personal guarantees from the directors (who could then be made bankrupt if the debts weren't paid).

Setting up and running a company involves various legal niceties and costs which a solicitor or accountant will help you sort out. In return for the protection of limited liability, the company must produce audited accounts (an extra cost) and file them at Companies House. There they are open for public inspection so that people who do business with you can check that you are creditworthy (as can any busybody or business rival).

SECTION 3

IS THE BUSINESS VIABLE?

No business can survive for long unless it is profitable. But at least as important is that the business should have enough cash to pay the bills before the profits start to roll in. This section explains how to check the finances before you start on your own, beginning with a business plan which sets out in detail exactly what you propose to do. It also includes brief details on whom to turn to if you need to borrow money, either to buy major items like premises or equipment, or to finance day-to-day working.

PLANNING FOR YOUR BUSINESS

You may have a fairly good idea in your own mind about the sort of business you intend to start and how it will run. You may even have made some 'back-of-an-envelope' calculations to prove to yourself that you can make a go of it. But it is essential to draw up a written business plan which sets out all the facts and assumptions and works through the figures in detail. Apart from helping you to spot possible pitfalls and problems in advance, a formal business plan will be essential if you need to borrow money to get started (even if only a bank overdraft).

A business plan should aim to achieve two objectives:

- an explanation of exactly what your business will do, why you think you will be successful, how you will achieve success and your qualifications for making it a success
- detailed figures to show that it will be profitable and that it won't run out of money before the profits come in, together with evidence to substantiate these figures. If money will have to be borrowed to achieve success, then these figures should show how much is needed and that the business will make enough money to pay the interest and repay the loan (if necessary).

The checklist opposite lists the sort of headings which should appear in a business plan. Naturally some headings will not apply to all businesses, but it is a useful checklist. If you are using an accountant, he or she should be involved in producing the business plan (especially the financial figures). But if you have thought through your plans before asking for the accountant's help, it should reduce the size of the bill! And it is important that the plan accurately reflects *your* intentions and that you can defend it if asked by the bank manager or anyone else whose help is needed.

The business plan is your first marketing document – the first attempt to sell your idea to others. A well-written, well-presented plan will say a lot about your abilities and intentions as well as helping you to think through what it is you want to do. Even cheap home computers can produce clean typescript and tables of figures (perhaps also bar charts and pie diagrams without too much difficulty) – see page 16 for more about computers. Give all the detail which you would want to know if you were asked to invest in someone else's business, but don't waffle on and pad it out: a short two-page summary followed by 10 to 12 pages of detail would be ideal.

FINANCIAL FORECASTS

A business should always prepare financial forecasts for the year ahead; in some cases, it is advisable to produce projections (with less detail) for one or two years further ahead. For the year ahead, forecasts should be prepared on a monthly basis, though with very simple

Business plan checklist

Background
- your personal history and experience
- objectives of the business
- the form of business (sole trader, partnership, company)
- some ideas of long-term strategy (e.g. to remain a single outlet, to expand or whatever)

The product or service
- a clear description (especially if it is specialised)
- any unique aspect you bring to it
- how it might develop

The market for your product or service
- where you will sell it
- numbers of potential customers (and why they will want it)
- competitors (and why you will beat them)
- how you will market your product or service

The team
- your skills, training and capabilities (even if it is just you)
- any key partners/employees (especially if they have crucial skills)
- details of any backers
- your professional advisers (accountant, bank, solicitor)
- how you will cope with unfamiliar aspects (e.g. accounts)
- pay details

Customers and suppliers
- details of who these are, especially where you sell to other businesses or need specialised supplies
- terms for trade with customers and suppliers, including payment arrangements

Premises and equipment
- where your business will be (and suitability of location)
- costs of premises and details of lease, service agreement etc.
- equipment, furniture and fittings – costs and where they will come from

Legal matters
- patents, trademarks, registered designs, copyright
- franchising arrangements, service agreements, guarantees, indemnities etc.
- leases for property, vehicles or equipment (terms and costs)

Financial projections
- profit and loss forecast
- cash flow forecast
- balance sheet (where applicable) PLUS detailed explanations of the assumptions (e.g. sales forecasts, inflation assumptions, interest rates, payment times)
- if possible, give break-even points (i.e. sales needed to reach a profit), and show what will happen on less optimistic assumptions (e.g. sales targets aren't met, or inflation rises)

Financial needs
- capital needed for premises, equipment etc. – and where it will come from
- working capital needed to pay wages, suppliers etc. before receipts come in – and where it will come from
- what you are putting in
- any security which can be offered for loans– property, investments etc.

businesses involving only a few transactions, quarterly figures would be enough. Apart from helping to see whether the business will succeed (on paper), these forecasts should be compared with what actually happens as the business progresses to identify problems and avoid unexpected crises.

There are two types of forecast to make:

- profit and loss – this tells you whether the business will make more in receipts than it pays out in costs and thus be profitable
- cash flow – even though the business is set to make a profit, the money from sales may not come in fast enough to pay the bills. If it doesn't, even a profitable enterprise can run out of money and go out of business.

There are blank worksheets to help you make both sorts of forecast in the back pocket of this Pack. Use a soft lead pencil when filling these in: you may have to alter the figures as you go along. If you can use a simple computer spreadsheet to do the forecasts, it will work out all the arithmetic for you, quickly incorporate changes and let you see what happens if your assumptions change.

Profit and loss forecast

Start by working out a set of monthly sales targets. Normally this will build up month by month, but there may be seasonal variations to think about (not least if you expect to have a holiday). Producing these sales involves two sorts of costs:

- *direct costs* which depend on the amount of sales. For example, if you make pine desks, doubling your sales will double the amount of the timber you have to use – so timber is a direct cost
- *overheads* – fixed costs which have to be paid irrespective of the level of sales, such as for premises, rates, insurance premiums and so on.

It's not always quite so clear-cut as this. For example, electricity is normally included in overheads, though you may use extra if sales go up. And while wage costs mightn't go up or down to match sales (especially if you employ just one person), production wages are usually described as a direct cost.

So the next step is to work out the direct cost of your sales for each month, based on the cost of raw materials and labour. If you don't employ anyone (e.g. you are a plumber working on your own or a freelance sub-editor), there may be no direct labour costs. And if you recharge your customers for the goods you supply to them (for example paint and wallpaper), there will be no costs for materials used. Most types of business will have some direct costs, however. If you employ people to make the product or provide the service, add their monthly wages and employment costs

(e.g. employer's National Insurance contributions and fringe benefits). With raw materials, you may be able to work on an average figure for each sale – for example, that each £100 of sales means an extra £25 of bills for raw materials.

Don't just use the amounts you actually pay out in any month for raw materials as this might give a misleading view of your costs: some of what you pay for might not be used in that month and go into your stock for the future; or you might be drawing from stock, appearing to reduce your costs artificially. The example below shows how to work out the cost of materials used in any month.

Monthly cost of sales	
Value of stock at beginning of month (A)	£1,200
Purchases of stock in month (B)	£200
Value of stock at end of month (C)	£1,100
Cost of materials used in month (A+B − C)	£300

Deducting direct costs from your sales receipts gives you your *gross profit*. Next work out the overhead fixed costs you might expect to pay, including premises, administration costs, insurance, advertising, bank charges and interest on loans. There are some wage costs you may wish to include as overheads, such as any amount you draw for yourself, payment to a sales rep (though his or her commission would be a direct cost), and wages for a secretary, book-keeper or delivery driver.

If you use expensive machinery, vehicles, computer or other equipment in your business, you shouldn't include the cost of buying them in your profit and loss forecast. Instead, include a figure for depreciation in the overheads to spread the cost of buying these capital items over the years that you use them. The amount you allow for depreciation depends on how much the item cost and how long you expect it to last. For example, a personal computer and printer for correspondence, accounts and design work costing £2,000 might last four years: this could give a depreciation allowance of ¼ of £2,000 = £500 a year.

If an overhead is paid only once or twice a year, you should average the cost across the whole year. For a simple business, you might find it easiest to add up all the overheads for the year and use an average monthly figure. The figure after deducting overheads is the *net profit* or *net loss*. It would not be unusual for the first months of a forecast to show a net loss, but sooner or later it must turn into a profit and the profits must outweigh earlier losses if the business is to be viable.

If you are registered for VAT, do not include VAT in the amounts for sales and purchases. If you are not registered for VAT, include VAT on your purchases (you shouldn't be charging it on sales!).

Cash flow forecast

A cash flow forecast tries to analyse when money will come into your business and when it will flow out. Money comes in from sales, and in most types of business this is usually some time after the sale is made. Money flows out to pay wages, rent, rates, bills for raw materials, overheads and so on – and these have to be paid even if the customer hasn't yet given you the money. If the gap is too large, you will need some working capital to pay your staff, yourself, your suppliers and your overheads before your customers cough up. The cash flow forecast helps you decide how much and when to put it into the business.

Start with receipts from sales: unless you are very lucky and get paid in advance, these will come in after the sale is made. Deciding how long after is a key assumption to make: even if you specify payment within (say) 30 days, some payments will come in later. For many businesses, getting the money in during the second month following the month of sale would be good going: so if you sold £1,000 of goods in January, on average you'd receive £1,000 in March.

Then fill in details of the payments you must make. Some will be in advance (for example, insurance premiums and purchases of equipment); some as you go along (wages, raw materials and so on); and some in quarterly or annual arrears (electricity and accountancy fees, for example). An accurate cash flow forecast must assign the right payments to the right month.

Some points to bear in mind:

- after-tax wages are paid in the week or month they are earned, but the tax and National Insurance you deduct under PAYE is handed over to the Inland Revenue in the following month (see page 31)
- when you pay suppliers depends on the terms you negotiate with them (e.g. monthly in arrears)
- you can pay business rates in ten equal instalments
- include VAT in the cost of purchases and sales even if you are registered for VAT. Any excess you have charged over what you have paid must be handed over to Customs and Excise quarterly (page 19)
- you may still need to estimate average outlays on things like travel and advertising.

The general rule of cash flow forecasting is that receipts usually come in later than you expect and are less than forecast; bills always end up being bigger than forecast and must always be paid on time!

FINANCE FOR THE BUSINESS

If your business needs to invest in premises or equipment, finance will be needed for this capital expenditure. But making the cash flow forecasts will often show that finance is needed to provide working capital to cover the gap between receipts and payments. There are six main sources of finance to consider:

- *personal finance you put in* (lenders will expect some sort of commitment from you before agreeing a loan)
- *bank loans* (or loans from similar lending institutions) – they will normally want to secure loans on any

business assets or with personal guarantees from you (so you go bankrupt if they're not paid)
- *bank overdraft* – usually cheaper than a loan, because you pay interest only on the amount by which you are overdrawn, not the full loan. An overdraft facility is always useful even if you hope not to use it, and especially suitable if you know that there will be periods of the year when you need to go into the red
- *venture capital* – usually put up by special investment companies for businesses they think will grow. The investor buys a stake in the firm and expects to sell it at a great profit when the business has taken off, so there may be little or no interest to pay in the meantime
- *investments by friends or family* – they may be able to get tax relief through the Business Expansion Scheme (see below)
- *grants from local authorities, the Government or the European Community* – not easily available, but always worth exploring, particularly if you are starting up in an area of high unemployment where funds are provided for regeneration. Details of national and EC funds from the Department of Trade and Industry (telephone Freefone Enterprise).

If you are seeking large amounts of finance, it is essential to discuss the possible sources with an accountant, who can also advise on the most tax-effective ways to borrow and the right mixture of finance for your business. You may be able to reduce the amount you need to borrow by leasing equipment rather than buying it. For certain types of business, factoring can help with finance: you hand over your sales invoices to a factoring company which pays you 80 per cent (say) of the amount you are owed straight away and chases the customer for the rest, generally keeping 5 per cent for the service.

Interest rates charged to small businesses are often higher than those charged to the big blue-chip companies, to reflect the extra risks involved. And the lender will want as much reassurance as possible about repayment, often including personal guarantees from you as owner and perhaps a second charge on your home (so if your business fails, you could lose your home). Finding sufficient guarantees can be difficult, and the Government Small Business Loan Guarantee Scheme can help where you have committed all your personal assets as security. The Scheme then guarantees 70 per cent of loans up to £100,000 for a charge of 2.5 per cent a year of the guaranteed part (with a simplified procedure for smaller loans). Up to 85 per cent of the loan can be guaranteed in certain inner-city areas. A booklet on the Scheme is available from Training and Enterprise Councils (TECs).

Business Expansion Scheme

Individuals who invest in the shares of new and growing businesses in the UK may be able to get tax relief on their investment through the Business Expansion Scheme (BES). The tax relief is at the investor's highest rate of tax, on up to £40,000 a year of BES investments (husband and wife can each get this much tax relief). And if you hold the shares for at least five years, the gain can be free of capital gains tax. If you think that investors in your business could benefit, ask your accountant for advice (there's an Inland Revenue booklet IR 51 *The Business Expansion Scheme*).

SECTION 4

RUNNING THE BUSINESS

Working for an employer usually means that there's someone else to take care of the day-to-day running of the business – the finances, advertising, finding premises and so on. When you work for yourself, you have to see to these matters on top of all the other responsibilities of self-employment. If you don't, your business could be at risk.

BUSINESS NAME

Many self-employed people trade under their own names ('Joanna Soap', 'Jerry Doe Ltd' or 'Soap, Doe and Byrne'). But you may prefer to use a name which attracts attention or says something about the business ('The Perfect Pickle', say, or 'Tahitian Textiles') – and within certain limits, you are free to do this. Useful booklets setting out the rules are available from Companies House. The main restrictions are on words which:

- imply national or international pre-eminence, like 'British' or 'European'
- suggest government or royal patronage, like 'Authority' or 'Royal'
- imply representative status, like 'Association' or 'Society'
- carry connotations of specific functions such as 'Insurance', 'Pharmacy', 'Charity' or 'Health Centre'.

It is illegal to pass yourself or your business off as something which it is not (for example, if you sold clothes and called yourself Marks & Spencer). Where you or your company use a business name, the surname(s) and business address(es) of the owner(s) (or the registered company name) must be prominently displayed wherever customers or suppliers might come in. Similar information must be given on business stationery.

A company registration agent will advise if you are forming a limited company.

BANK ACCOUNTS

Even if you are working as a sole trader and on your own, you should still open a special bank account for the business. All income from the business should be paid into this account, and purchases paid for using cheques drawn on it. Keeping your business finances separate from your personal finances has several advantages:

- it makes it easier to draw up the annual accounts for the Inland Revenue (and for VAT if registered) and to show that you have declared all your income
- you can claim any bank charges on a business account as an allowable expense against tax (see page 25)
- it will make it easier to borrow money from the bank to buy equipment or to finance your day-to-day working.

Ask to see your bank manager when you open the business account and discuss your plans with him. The bank will offer a variety of services to small businesses, including night safe deposit boxes to pay in cash outside working hours, cash cards and business credit cards, help from specialist small business advisers and various types of business loan.

DECIDING YOUR TERMS OF TRADE

When you sell goods or services, there is a contract between you and your customer. The same applies when you order goods from a supplier. If there is no written contract, the deal is covered by business legislation and common law. But you can draw up a formal written contract to specify, for example, payment periods, methods of payment, cancellation clauses, delivery deadlines and so on.

In some types of business, there are standard terms and conditions which most people expect to apply – though this must be spelt out when the deal is agreed (for example, by incorporating them into the quotation). In others, no such formal document is needed, but it is still wise to include some basic conditions in setting out your proposal (for example, for payment within one month). A solicitor should be able to advise on what is necessary; if there's a trade or professional association that covers your business, it may have standard terms and conditions to which you should stick.

Note that if you intend to give credit or hire out equipment to ordinary consumers, you may need to follow procedures set out in the Consumer Credit Act 1974. This includes drawing up formal agreements, quoting interest rates in a legally defined way and getting a licence from the Office of Fair Trading (OFT). You can get useful leaflets from the OFT on these requirements, including on licensing, credit charges and agreements.

PUTTING YOURSELF ON THE MAP

Unless you come from a marketing background, selling your business will be one skill you will have to learn. Useful books are available and there are plenty of courses on the subject (see page 6).

Some simple points to consider are:

- get some eye-catching notepaper printed (a local printer or copy shop should be able to do this for £100 or so). Certain information must be included on business stationery such as the surname(s) of the owner(s) if trading under a business name, the business address and details of the company registration with a limited company (see above)
- make sure your business is listed in the telephone directory, *Yellow Pages* and any relevant trade directories
- write to everyone you have ever worked with in your old job who might possibly need your product or service or who might be able to recommend you. Personal contact and recommendation are almost invariably the best sources of custom
- consider advertising in the local press. A classified advertisement may be the first – not unduly expensive – step, followed by more ambitious advertising if appropriate. Small local advertising agencies can advise
- see if you can get free advertising in the local papers, if only by press releasing your launch. An official office opening by a local bigwig or some newsworthy stunt (especially if it also raises money for charity) can give you helpful press coverage.

Other ideas include mailshots to possible customers and 'cold calling' (ringing them up to introduce yourself). It's a good idea to have a brochure or examples of your work to show, and some sort of visual reminder to leave with people you meet (business card, jotting pad, pen with your name on, calendar or whatever).

PREMISES

The premises you need depend on your line of business. Many small businesses need no special premises – their owners work from home or in their customers' homes or workplaces. With others, the choice of premises can be crucial to success.

Whether you work from home or special premises, you will need to look into planning restrictions on the business use of your workplace. There's a useful free booklet *A Step-by-Step Guide to Planning Permission for Small Businesses* prepared for England and Wales by the Department of the Environment and Welsh Office. A companion booklet sets out the special rules for advertisements: *Outdoor Advertisements and Signs: a Guide for Advertisers.*

Working from home

Many people starting up in business will begin by working from home. This saves money on rent, business rates, heating etc., and is often more convenient (no journey to work, someone to answer the telephone and so on).

But working from home may need planning permission if it involves a change of use from residential to business purposes. This depends on the sort of work: small-scale handicrafts or using the home as an office base is unlikely to need permission, but any of the following could mean that you must apply to the local planning authority:

- using more than one room for the business activity
- using more than one machine (or set of machinery)
- employing people at your home
- making a lot of noise or disturbance that will affect the neighbours
- attracting numbers of callers or deliveries
- displaying external advertising signs.

Using your garage to store materials or even parking a trade van on your drive may need planning permission. Broadly, if no-one is likely to notice that you are working from home, you are unlikely to need planning permission (your local planning authority will offer guidance). If planning permission is needed, it may be granted only subject to certain conditions to reduce noise and disturbance – limits on working hours, for example. Even where planning permission isn't required, restrictions may be imposed on business use of your home by the terms of its lease or by restrictive covenants.

Special business premises

Working from home probably won't be an option if you're engaged in larger-scale manufacture, employing people or offering direct access to the public. You will need some sort of workshop, factory, office or shop which is not only suitable for the use you have in mind but also has planning permission for it.

For example, while you don't need permission to convert a clothes shop into a hairdresser's, you do need permission to convert it into an insurance broking office. And even industrial premises may need planning permission to be used for certain types of manufacturing or warehousing. Make sure that you can use the premises as you intend before signing any agreement to buy or lease it.

Other points to consider when searching for business premises include:

- is there sufficient space not only for now, but for the next two or three years, to avoid the upheaval of moving to larger premises too soon?
- is there adequate access for customers, staff, deliveries and collections (especially where lorries are involved)?
- what is the total cost – rent, rates, insurance, waste removal, service charges etc.? Is a premium required (a lump sum payment to buy the lease)? Are there regular rent reviews?
- is there adequate security, sound insulation, drainage, storage, floor loading and ceiling heights?
- are there convenient ancillary services such as catering, photocopying, transport?
- what are your obligations as tenant (e.g. to repair and decorate)?
- is there a fire certificate (if needed)?
- can you dispose of the lease if you need to move (or the business fails)?

A good place to start looking for premises is with the local council which may maintain a register of vacant premises to encourage new businesses to open up. Local estate agents also handle business property, though small units may be advertised directly by placards or in the local press. Sub-letting from someone with spare capacity can be a cheap option (and you could share overheads and facilities). Serviced office accommodation can also give you access to a shared photocopier, fax and receptionist. Premises in an enterprise zone may be particularly cheap, with no rates to pay for the first few years. And there are special deals in assisted areas with high unemployment. The advice of a solicitor is essential in finding premises and arranging terms. Get a surveyor to look at the premises before you sign anything, especially if you will be liable for repairs and improvements. And check the taxation implications with your accountant – the rules depend on the type of lease and how long it has to run.

You should also ask your solicitor for advice about health and safety provisions, especially if you employ staff or use hazardous processes. Guidance is available on these matters from the Health and Safety Executive.

INSURANCE

Even if you plan to work entirely on your own from home, you must look at your existing insurance policies and consider additional ones. And if you intend to employ people or start a more ambitious business, special insurance policies should be considered.

You should:

- notify your existing insurers about your change of job, especially if you plan to use your home or car for work. Your household and car insurance policies may not pay out if you have not told the companies you are self-employed
- look at the amount of life insurance cover you've got, especially if you previously relied on life insurance provided at work as a fringe benefit
- consider permanent health insurance, which pays out an income if you can't work through illness or injury
- take out employer's liability cover if you employ people – it's compulsory to have it and to display the insurance certificate at the place of work
- insure your business premises and their contents (including stock) against fire, flood, theft etc., with cover for goods in transit, money on its way to the bank and loss of earnings in case of one of these disasters
- take out special insurance for any business vehicles and their drivers
- consider insurance against claims for professional negligence or damage or injury caused by your product or service
- consider legal expenses insurance towards the cost of legal advice and representation (if people fail to meet delivery deadlines, say, or you are taken to an industrial tribunal).

An insurance broker who is experienced in business insurance will arrange these policies for you at no charge (the broker earns commission on the policies from the insurance companies).

COMPUTERS

Many small businesses find personal computers invaluable for:

- word-processing standard letters, personalised mailshots, attractive reports and proposals, order forms, price lists etc. (desktop publishing can produce even more attractive results)
- keeping accounts, producing invoices and reminders, and generating financial reports
- financial forecasting with spreadsheets which allow you to produce accurate forecasts of profit and loss and cash flow, and to test changes in assumptions (e.g. prices)
- databases to keep details of stock items, prices, customers or subscribers and so on.

A simple system capable of most of the above applications can be bought for under £1,000 (an IBM-compatible computer and letter-quality dot matrix printer). For under £3,000 you can buy a state-of-the-art, reliable colour system with fast laser printer. Most good equipment now comes with a year's warranty covering parts and labour; a follow-up maintenance contract includes replacement equipment if yours is being repaired.

You also need software: the well-known software packages for word-processing, accounts and spreadsheet can cost nearly as much as the cheapest computer if bought on their own, but you can often get them more cheaply as part of a deal when buying the computer. And there are cheap integrated packages offering two or three uses in one, for sending letters to everyone on your client database, for example – these may be more than adequate for small business use. Training in how to use the best-known software packages is widely available from evening classes and commercial training firms.

The most difficult task for small businesses is choosing the right computer equipment and software, since most people offering advice want to sell you a limited range of products. There are independent computer consultants, but their charges can be hefty (though you might get free or cheap advice from one of the advisers mentioned on page 6). The Government-sponsored National Computing Centre has consultants specialising in advising small businesses. And there are 20 Microsystems Centres throughout the UK offering advice and training on computers to small businesses, for a fee. You may be able to get help with the cost from the Government's Enterprise Initiative – see page 6.

Data Protection Act

If you use computers to store or process 'personal data', you may have to register with the Data Protection Registrar. This will mean that your business is listed in a public register of data users and bureaux; you must follow a code of practice to keep the information secure, accurate and relevant to your needs; and you must reply to requests from people for details of any personal information you hold on them.

'Personal data' is information held on a computer about people, and registration is needed if what you keep is more than just the names, addresses and telephone numbers of customers, suppliers or anyone else. There's an exemption from registration for people who keep personal information purely for business accounts purposes – but you still have to register if you use the data for any other use (e.g. marketing) or you keep other data with it (e.g. information on credit limits).

The Data Protection Registrar has produced a detailed information pack.

PATENTS, SERVICE AND TRADE MARKS AND REGISTERED DESIGNS

These are all rights which can be established by owners of 'intellectual property', designed to protect the people who create bright ideas. If you want to use other people's bright ideas, you may need their permission if they have taken out one of these forms of protection – and you may have to pay for it. If the bright ideas are yours, you can stop people stealing your ideas, or to get payment for allowing others to use them.

You can register your ownership of a bright idea with an official body, the Patent Office:

- *taking out a patent* gives you the ownership and right to exploit a new invention for up to 20 years (subject to paying renewal fees from the fourth anniversary of filing). You must prove that your invention really is new, that it is an advance (rather than just an improvement) and that it is capable of being used in industry or agriculture
- *registering a design* gives you the ownership of the way an object looks for five years (renewable for four further five-year periods). The design must be new or original and cover an article manufactured in quantity
- *registering a trade mark* makes it easier to stop others copying it (it doesn't have to be registered). The first registration lasts for seven years and can be renewed at 14-year intervals indefinitely. A trade mark is a device (picture or logo), word or words, signature or some combination of these which is distinctive, not deceptive, not easily confused with other registered marks, does not describe or characterise the product (e.g. not 'tasty') and is not a geographical name or surname. A service mark is the equivalent of a trade mark for a service.

Information packs are available from the Patent Office for each of these. Registration involves completing a form, submitting details and paying a fee; after checking that ownership is not already

17

registered and (except with designs) a period for objections, registration goes ahead on payment of another fee. Registration can usually be extended on payment of further fees.

It would be worth discussing taking out a patent or registering a design or trade mark with a solicitor. A patent agent can help you in the process – the Chartered Institute of Patent Agents produces an explanatory leaflet. Note that protection can usually be extended abroad.

YOUR PENSION

One big difference between working for an employer and working for yourself is that you will have to give more thought to your pension. Not only is there no employer's pension scheme to provide you with a pension on retirement, as self-employed you cannot contribute to the State Earnings-Related Pension Scheme – SERPS (unless your business is a company). That means the only pension you can qualify for from the state is the flat-rate basic pension, unlikely to be enough to live on in retirement. You will have to contribute to a personal pension scheme if you want more than this basic minimum (if your business is a company, you could consider setting up some sort of company pension scheme).

With a personal pension scheme, you save towards a fund for your retirement, with regular instalments, one-off lump sums or both. You may get tax relief on your contributions (within generous limits – see below); and the fund your contributions go into pays no income tax or capital gains tax – so the money should grow faster than if you invested it yourself. At any time between your 50th and 75th birthdays you can start drawing a pension (you don't have to stop working). The pension is provided by using your accumulated fund to buy an annuity – the amount of income your fund buys depends on the size of the fund and interest rates at the time (the higher interest rates are, the more pension you'll get). You can take up to a quarter of your fund as a tax-free lump sum.

If you start to contribute to a personal pension only late on in your working life, you'll need to invest the maximum possible to get a reasonable pension. Start making contributions as soon as possible so that your fund can build up sufficiently by retirement. If you've contributed less than the maximum during the previous seven years, you may be able to make a contribution which is much bigger than the maximum for this year – for more details, see the current edition of *Which? Way to Save Tax*.

Limits on personal pension contributions 1991–2

Age on 6 April 1991	% of net relevant earnings*	maximum contribution**
35 or under	17½	£12,495
36–45	20	£14,280
46–50	25	£17,850
51–55	30	£21,420
56–60	35	£24,990
61 and over	40	£28,560

* Your net relevant earnings are:
- if you are a director or employee – earnings from non-pensionable jobs, including the taxable value of fringe benefits but excluding allowable expenses
- if you are self-employed – your taxable profits, less certain payments made by your business after deduction of tax such as patent royalties.

** Based on the pension scheme earnings cap of £71,400 for 1991–2

Pensions from employment

If you've previously worked for an employer, you may have built up some entitlement to a pension from the employer's scheme. This will probably be linked to your salary when you left the job, and increase by the lower of 5 per cent a year or the rate of inflation – so it may not add up to a huge sum by the time you come to retire. You should be able to transfer your pension rights from the employer's scheme to your personal pension if this looks to be preferable.

SECTION 5

VAT

VAT is often a subject of complaint for the self-employed, but it can't be overlooked when thinking about working for yourself. Registering for VAT can actually help your business by saving you money, since you will be able to claim back the VAT you pay on things you buy for your business – including items bought before starting it up.

On the other hand, if your business is small-scale, you probably won't need to worry about VAT. As a general rule of thumb, if the total value of what you expect to sell in a year is much less than £35,000 you don't need to get involved in VAT (though it may still be worthwhile to do so if you pay a lot of VAT on raw materials, equipment and so on).

There's a brief guide to VAT below, but this can only touch on a complicated subject. There are some helpful leaflets available from Customs and Excise VAT offices (under *Customs and Excise Department* in the telephone book) – listed below with the prefixes CE or VAT. The advice of an accountant may be essential (and the advice may save you more than it costs).

HOW VAT WORKS

VAT (Value Added Tax) is a tax on sales, collected for the government by HM Customs and Excise. When you buy goods and services, VAT is normally added to the cost. There are three categories of goods and services:

- *standard-rated*, on which VAT is currently added at $17\frac{1}{2}$ per cent – this applies to most goods and services
- *zero-rated*, on which VAT is currently charged at 0 per cent – mainly food from shops, books, newpapers and magazines, public transport, children's clothes and goods for export
- *exempt*, on which no VAT is payable – including insurance and other financial services, postage, most health care.

Some types of goods and services may fall into more than one category, according to their use. For example, heating and lighting is zero-rated for home use, but standard-rated for business use. And while new homes are zero-rated, business buildings and building repair work is standard-rated.

If your business is registered for VAT, you must add VAT at the correct rate to what you charge for everything you sell (this is called *output tax*). But you can claim back the VAT you pay (*input tax*) on most goods and services you buy for the business (the biggest exceptions are VAT on cars, business entertaining and some second-hand goods). Normally this is sorted out once every quarter:

- you add up the amount of tax you have charged on your sales for the period (even if you haven't yet been paid it)
- you add up the amount of VAT you have been charged on purchases for the period (even if you haven't yet paid the bills)
- if output tax exceeds input tax you hand over the difference to the Customs and Excise. If input tax exceeds output tax, you can claim back the difference.

Suppose that in one quarter you sold £5,000 of standard-rated goods. You would add VAT at $17\frac{1}{2}$ per cent to the bills – making £875 in output tax. If you had paid £1,000 for raw materials on which standard-rate VAT is charged, your input tax would be £175. At the end of the quarter, you would hand over the difference between output and input tax (£875 – £175 = £700) to Customs and Excise.

If you produce exempt goods or services, you don't charge VAT on them, but you can't claim back the input tax on them

19

either. So if your business is entirely exempt, you have to pay VAT on your telephone bill, electricity etc., without being able to claim it back. If your business is partially exempt – some of your outputs are exempt and some aren't – you may be able to claim back some or all of the input tax. If you think this might apply to you, get immediate advice from an accountant to minimise the amount of VAT you have to pay.

WHO NEEDS TO REGISTER FOR VAT?

Registration for VAT is compulsory if your *taxable turnover* reaches a level set by Parliament. Taxable turnover is the total value of goods and services you produce which are either standard-rated or zero-rated (i.e. exempt supplies don't count). If at the end of any month your taxable turnover for the past 12 months exceeds £35,000, you must register for VAT. The same applies if at any time you expect your taxable turnover for the next 30 days to exceed £35,000.

Once you realise that registration is necessary, contact your local VAT office. They will send you an introductory pack of leaflets, the *VAT Guide* (VAT 700) and forms VAT 1 and VAT 2 to fill in for registration (there's a copy of both these forms in the back pocket of this Pack). For VAT 1 you need to know the correct VAT classification code for your type of business: a full list appears in leaflet VAT 41 (also in the back pocket).

You must start adding VAT to your bills straight away, even before registration comes through. And you should keep proper VAT records showing the amount added – see below. Don't itemise VAT separately on your invoices until registration is through, but tell your customers that it is included: once registration comes through, issue duplicate invoices showing the VAT (and your VAT number), so that they can claim back the VAT if necessary.

Note that if you fail to register when it is compulsory, Customs and Excise can make you pay the VAT that would have been due – even though you haven't charged your customers for it. And you need to register even if you are buying a business from someone who is already registered for VAT: it is the person who registers, not the business. You can apply to register before buying the business (or before setting one up) to avoid delay.

CE 700/1 *Should I be Registered for VAT?*

Voluntary registration

Even if your taxable supplies are below the limit for compulsory registration, you can apply to be registered.

There can be advantages in registration: for example, you can claim back all your input tax, and if your product or service is zero-rated this will cut your costs without putting up your charges. And if you expect your business to grow to a size where registration will be required, it might be easier to register from the start – both for setting up the accounting system and so that your customers don't suddenly find an extra 17½ per cent on their bills.

Customs and Excise will agree to registration provided they are convinced that you are running a *bona fide* business – they don't want people registering for small amounts of freelance work in order to claim back the VAT on all sorts of expenses.

VAT before you register

One bonus of registering for VAT is that you may be able to claim back the VAT paid on goods and services you use in setting up your business. There are conditions to be met to qualify for this, however, so check with the *VAT Guide* to see if you can claim the tax back.

DEALING WITH VAT

After you have been registered, you are sent a certificate of registration, with your VAT number and date of registration.

You will also be told when the first set of accounts must be made up to – this may be a full quarter or perhaps only two months. If the end of a quarter won't coincide with the end of your accounting year, you can ask Customs and Excise to alter your VAT accounting quarters to fit.

Once your VAT registration is through, you should organise the paperwork to operate the VAT system. In particular, your invoices and credit notes must include:

- your name, address and VAT number
- a unique identifying number (retain any cancelled invoices or credit notes so that the sequence is not interrupted)
- the date the goods or services were supplied (the tax point)
- the customer's name and address
- details of the goods and services, including the quantity and charge excluding VAT
- the rate and amount of VAT
- the total charge excluding VAT and total VAT.

You must keep copies of all invoices you issue, and get and keep VAT invoices from your suppliers. Your accounts should record all taxable goods and services that you receive or supply – together with details of the VAT on them. If you use a computer accounting package, this will normally handle VAT automatically, but you should check with the VAT office that the package you use is acceptable to them.

Within a month of the end of each VAT accounting quarter, you must fill in the VAT return and send it off with any VAT you owe Customs and Excise for the period. All business records should be kept for six years.

CE 700/12 *Filling in your VAT Return*

CE 700/21 *Keeping Records and Accounts*

Enforcement

There are stiff penalties for failing to make VAT returns and payments on time. So it is vital to keep up to date with VAT.

You will be visited occasionally by a VAT officer, to check that you are operating the system correctly and keeping the right records. The first visit will normally be within 18 months of registration.

CE 700/26: *Visits by VAT officers*

SPECIAL SCHEMES

There are special schemes which can simplify VAT for small businesses. For example, if you sell direct to the public, various retail schemes avoid the need to issue a VAT invoice for every sale (see notice 727/6 *Choosing your Retail Scheme*).

If your taxable turnover excluding VAT is less than £300,000 a year, you can opt for a cash accounting basis. This means that the VAT you pay to Customs and Excise depends on the money you actually receive and pay out in the quarter, not what is invoiced. So you don't have to hand over VAT until you receive it from your customers – a great help if payment normally takes some time to come through. It also gives you VAT relief on bad debts, since unless you are paid, you don't have to hand over the VAT. More details in notice 731 *Cash Accounting*.

Also open to you if your taxable turnover is below £300,000 a year is the option to make annual VAT returns, rather than quarterly ones. You must have been registered for a year before this is allowed: your VAT bill for the coming year is estimated and collected by direct debit in nine monthly instalments; when the annual return is completed, the balance is due (or a repayment made to you). More details in notice 732 *Annual Accounts*.

Finally, if your business produces zero-rated goods or services, you will normally get a refund of input VAT at the end of each quarter, rather than having to make a payment to Customs and Excise. You can ask for monthly VAT accounting periods instead of quarterly ones to get the money back more quickly (though this means filling in more forms).

SECTION

ACCOUNTS AND INCOME TAX

Even the smallest business must keep accounts of the money coming in and going out, if only to satisfy the tax authorities. But accurate accounts will also help you monitor the health of your business and alert you to problems which would otherwise creep up on you.

KEEPING ACCOUNTS

The accounts you need to keep will depend on the business. You can buy printed account books for small businesses which may be suitable for your business, or you can buy blank ledgers and mug up on simple accounting methods for yourself. If you are at all unsure about accounts, ask your accountant to set up a system and teach you how to use it. If you follow this system, it will make it easier to produce regular accounts.

Some basic points to remember in dealing with your accounts are:

- always try to collect a written record of any transaction, even if it is only a till roll or note on the back of an envelope
- never throw any paperwork away unless you are certain it is unnecessary – keep copies of invoices you issue invoices you are sent, cheque-book stubs, bank statements, receipts for cash payments etc.
- keep a petty cash book to record small out-of-pocket expenses
- if you employ people, keep a separate wages book to record their pay, income tax, National Insurance contributions etc. (you can buy pre-printed ones)
- keep paid invoices separate from unpaid ones, so that you can quickly gauge what you owe and are owed
- if you are registered for VAT, there must be a special VAT column in all your records.

A simple system

For the simplest businesses you can probably base everything on a cash book. This records all your payments and receipts made by cheque or ready money.

It is best to use a specially printed analysis book, which you can buy with a variety of numbers of columns. Use these columns to record different types of payment and receipt: for example, you can separate purchases of raw materials and other direct costs from overheads, costs of premises from administration and so on. Enter the payments and receipts in date order.

At the end of each month, add up the totals of income and expenditure to see what the 'bottom line' is – your cash balance. Check the figure against your monthly bank statement (this is called the *bank reconciliation*). If there is a difference, it should be equal to the total of cheques you have sent out which have yet to be presented and amounts you have paid into the bank which have not yet been cleared.

When you have balanced the books, compare what has happened with your cash flow forecast for the month. If reality differs from your forecast, try to analyse why by looking at the figures that vary (the *variances*, as your accountant will put it). It may be something that will sort itself out later (a late payment, say), or a more fundamental problem that means you must revise your forecast.

Keeping an eye on outstanding bills

The cash balance needs to be looked at beside any bills you have not yet paid and any invoices you have issued which have yet to be paid. If there are a lot of these,

22

you should keep two further books: a sales day book to record your sales invoices as they are sent out (and when payment is received); and a purchases day book to record your purchases of goods and services (and when you pay them off).

Check the sales day book from time to time to make sure that you are being paid for the work you do, and chase up late payments. If you have been offered discount for prompt payment for goods and services, use the purchases day book to make sure you don't lose out by making the payments too late.

More advanced accounts

In all but the smallest businesses, you will graduate to keeping ledgers which use the system of double-entry book-keeping:

- a sales ledger, to which you transfer information from the sales day book to produce an individual record for each customer (or class of business)
- a purchases ledger, which does the same for each of your suppliers
- a nominal ledger (or general ledger), which brings the two together under headings like debtors, creditors, bank balance, sales, wages and so on.

At the end of the year, you draw up a balance sheet, which shows the resources of your business: the assets (what it owns, money in the bank, money owed etc.); and the liabilities (money you owe suppliers or have borrowed, overdraft etc.).

Simple and inexpensive accounts software can be bought for use on a personal computer which looks after this book-keeping. Check with your accountant before going too far with buying a computer accounts package.

Quarterly accounts

Balance the figures monthly so that you can sort out any mistakes easily, and make deeper checks at least once every quarter.

In particular, you or your accountant should prepare a quarterly profit and loss account (using the same approach as on page 10). Compare it with your forecast – if it is different, try to analyse why. For example, the gross profit tells you whether you are covering the cost of labour and materials in each sale. If your margin (gross profit as a percentage of sales) is lower than expected, find out why. Or are your overheads higher than expected – can you trim them?

At the same time review your cash flow against forecast. It may be that you were too optimistic about how quickly you would be paid or how much stock of raw materials you would build up. Checking the figures will help you raise any extra finance in time to keep going. And a couple of hours' telephoning people who owe you money might transform the position if you find that late payment is a problem.

INCOME TAX ON YOUR PROFITS

If you are working for yourself as a sole trader or in a partnership, the profits of the business will be liable to income tax under Schedule D, irrespective of any money you draw from it. There's more about income tax in the most recent editions of *Which? Way to Save Tax* and the *Which? Tax-saving Guide*, and the Inland Revenue produces useful leaflets on some tax matters (listed below with the IR prefix).

Note that if your business is a company, corporation tax is paid on the profits. Your salary from the company will be taxed in much the same way as any other employee's, under PAYE (see page 31). If you draw dividends, advance corporation tax must be paid on them. While the principles of corporation tax are more or less the same as for income tax, there are important practical differences. Your accountant will advise you on this.

IR 57: *Thinking of Working for Yourself?*

Starting your business

As soon as you start a business, you should notify the Inspector of Taxes for the area where you are trading (under *Inland Revenue – Taxes, HM Inspectors of* in the telephone book). You can do this with Inland Revenue form 41G, a copy of which is included in the back pocket of this Pack. Ask for a copy of booklet IR 28 *Starting in Business*, which has plenty of useful advice and a list of other leaflets on matters such as the Business Expansion Scheme (see page 12) and PAYE (if you employ people).

If you were previously in paid employment, send your P45 from your former employer to the new tax office, which should normally offer you a refund of tax. There will be no tax assessment on your business profits until you have been in business for at least a year. Once you have completed your first accounting year, you will start to get tax bills for your profits.

Accounting year

A business's accounts are normally made up annually to the same day each year – your annual accounting date or the end of your accounting year. This accounting year need not run from 1 January to 31 December, nor need it coincide with the tax year (from 6 April in one year to 5 April in the next). And it doesn't have to be the 12 months after you start trading – your first accounting year can be more (or less) than 12 months.

In fact, because of the way that profits are taxed, there can be considerable benefits in choosing the right accounting year. As a general rule, the tax you pay on business profits in any tax year depends on your taxable profits in the accounting year which ended in the previous tax year. This is known as a preceding-year basis of assessment: the tax you pay in the 1991–2 tax year (which began on 6 April 1991) depends on the profits you made in the accounting year which ended in the 1990–1 tax year. The tax is due in two instalments, on 1 January in the middle of the tax year and on 1 July following the end of the tax year.

So if your accounting year ended on 30 April in each year, the tax bill for 1991–2 would depend on the profits in your accounting year ending on 30 April 1990. The first tax payment would be due on 1 January 1992 – 20 months after the end of the accounting year. If your accounting year ended on 31 March, by contrast, the first tax due on the profits in that year would be due just nine months later.

Once you have chosen an accounting year, it is not easy to change it. Consider the options carefully and get advice from your accountant. There are special rules for assessing the business profits for tax in the first three years of a new business.

IR 26: *Income Tax Assessments on Business Profits – Changes of Accounting Date*

Assessing your tax bill

Your accounts will form the basis of your tax assessment, and the tax inspector has the right to go through your books. Normally, he or she will want to see your profit and loss account, the trading account if there is one, and sometimes the balance sheet. If you don't produce acceptable accounts, the inspector may estimate your tax bill, and you will have to pay the estimated tax bill unless you can prove that it is excessive.

An accountant will know the best way to present your accounts, and be able to work out the various allowances and adjustments which decide the final tax bill. The tax inspector will normally write directly to your accountant; tax returns and notices of assessment will still come to you, though you can ask for copies of notices of assessment to be sent to your accountant.

If your business is a simple one, you may be able to do this for yourself with the help of a good tax guide. And if your total turnover is less than £10,000 a year, you can submit simplified 'three-line accounts' without any detail (though the tax inspector can ask to see the detail).

IR 104: *Simple Tax Accounts*

Taxable profits

You are taxed on your taxable profits for your accounting year. These are broadly your takings for the year less allowable business expenses, but some or all of the following adjustments are made:

- *include* any change in value of your stocks during the year (see overleaf)
- *deduct* money owed to you at the start of the accounting year, and *add* money owed to you at the end of the year for goods and services that you've supplied (see overleaf)
- *add* money which you owe to someone else at the start of the accounting year and *deduct* money you owe at the end of the accounting year, for purchases you've made and business expenses.

You can also make the following adjustments when calculating the amount of your income from all sources on which you'll have to pay tax:

- *deduct* capital allowances (see overleaf)
- *deduct* half the amount of any Class 4 National Insurance contributions you pay in the year of assessment (page 27)
- *deduct* losses (page 27).

If you have worked out your trading profit as described on page 10, you can start from this figure to calculate your taxable profits. Broadly, you add to your trading profit any expenses which are not allowable for income tax (for example, entertaining expenses, depreciation) and subtract capital allowances and any losses you can claim for tax purposes.

IR 105: *How your Profits are Taxed*

Allowable business expenses

You can deduct allowable business expenses from your profits. An expense will be allowable only if it is incurred 'wholly and exclusively' for the business, and what you can claim will depend on the type of business. The cost of the following items is generally allowed (include VAT if you are not a VAT-registered trader):

- wages of staff and benefits for them such as pensions and life insurance (including for any members of your family if genuinely employed in the business and if the wages and benefits are commensurate with the work done)
- raw materials and goods bought for resale
- rent and rates on business premises
- telephone, heating, lighting, water rates for premises used by the business
- business travel (though not between your home and main place of work)
- advertising, delivery charges, stationery, postage and other administrative expenses
- premiums for business insurance (but not your own life, accident or sickness insurance policies)
- interest on business loans, including on hire purchase of equipment
- equipment rental
- accountancy fees, bank charges and legal costs (including fees to register a trade mark, design or patent)
- subscriptions to trade and professional associations.

Among the expenses not normally allowed are your own wages or salary, ordinary clothing, business entertaining, gifts costing more than £10 a year per person to anyone other than employees, fines, tax penalties and surcharges, and payments to political parties. Depreciation on plant, equipment and vehicles and capital expenditure – including buildings, the cost of buying a patent, and alterations and improvements to premises – are also not allowed, though you may be able to claim capital allowances (see overleaf).

If your house, car or telephone is used partly for your business, you may claim a proportion of its costs. The proportion depends on the degree of business usage and must normally be agreed with the tax inspector. For example, you could claim the proportion of your car expenses corresponding to the proportion of your total mileage that is for business use (this means keeping a record of business mileage). With home expenses, the proportion of bills such as rent, insurance and fuel you can claim might depend on the number and size of rooms you use for business and the period used. But if you use part of your home *exclusively* for business, there may be some capital gains tax to pay when you sell the home. Note that you cannot claim as a business expense the personal community charge (poll tax) you pay at your main home; you may be able to claim a proportion of the standard community charge payable on a second home if it is partly let out or used for business.

Raw materials and stocks

You can claim as an allowable expense the cost of raw materials and of things you buy for resale. But you can claim only the cost of materials which you actually sell during your accounting year – i.e. the value of your stocks at the start of the year (*opening stock value*), plus anything you spend on buying more during that year, minus the value of your stocks at the end of the year (*closing stock value*).

A stock-take, therefore, is essential at the end of your accounting year. A decrease in stocks reduces your taxable profits for the year, while an increase normally boosts them.

Money owed

Money owed *to* your business at the end of your accounting year counts as part of the income for the business – even though you haven't in fact received it. The cost of allowable expenses can be deducted from your profits even if you haven't yet paid the bills. So when working out your taxable profits, don't include amounts you've received (or paid) to settle debts from earlier years.

If you decide in a later tax year – and the inspector agrees – that a debt is not going to be paid, you can count this bad debt as an allowable expense.

Capital allowances

Capital expenditure is money spent on plant, machinery, vehicles, buildings and anything else which has an enduring benefit for the business and does not need to be renewed every year. It is not, in itself, tax deductible but you can claim capital allowances to set off against your taxable profits. For items bought partly for business and partly for private use, you get a proportion of the maximum capital allowances in line with business use.

The cost of plant, machinery or business vehicles such as vans and lorries goes into a *pool of expenditure*. At the end of each accounting year, you can claim up to 25 per cent of the value of your pool of expenditure as a *writing-down allowance*, and deduct that amount from your profits. The pool is reduced by what you claim; what's left is known as the *written-down value*. Note that you don't have to claim the full 25 per cent writing-down allowance: anything unclaimed is carried forward to next year's pool of expenditure and can reduce your tax in later years.

If you sell something on which you have claimed capital allowances, its value (usually the sale proceeds) must be deducted from your pool before working out your writing-down allowance for the year. If the proceeds come to more than the value of your pool, the excess (the *balancing charge*) is added to your profits.

You must have a separate pool of expenditure for assets bought partly for business and partly for private use and for cars (any car costing over £8,000 has its own separate pool, with a maximum writing-down allowance of £2,000 in any year). There are special rules for capital allowances for buildings, for equipment which you expect to sell or scrap within five years (computers, for example), and in the opening and closing years of a business – ask your accountant.

IR 106: *Capital Allowances for Vehicles and Machinery*

Losses

If you make a taxable profit, there may be income tax to pay on it. But if you make a tax loss – your deductions exceed your takings – you may be able to claim back tax paid on other types of income or on your business profits in previous tax years or future ones.

There are three choices about how to set a business loss off against tax:

- against future profits from the same business
- against other income taxable in the following tax year – such as income from employment or income from investments (anything left over is set against income from the same business)
- against other income for the tax year in which your accounting year ends – this could include profits made in the previous accounting year (see page 24).

Losses you make in the first four tax years of your business may be set against wages or other income in the three years before the loss was incurred. So tax paid in those years will then be refunded, from the earliest year's income first – providing a repayment from the Inland Revenue.

Making the best use of losses requires skill and thought – consult your accountant on how to maximise the tax you save.

NATIONAL INSURANCE

As a sole trader or partner, you must pay Class 2 National Insurance contributions, and probably also Class 4 contributions. DSS leaflet NI 41 *National Insurance for Self-employed People* in the back pocket of this Pack sets out the rules. Note that if your business is a company, you will count as an employee and pay Class 1 contributions – see page 32.

Although the self-employed pay National Insurance contributions, they are not eligible for certain state benefits, including unemployment benefit and sickness benefit. And while paying Class 2 contributions counts towards the flat-rate state basic pension, self-employed National Insurance contributions do not count towards the State Earnings-Related Pension Scheme (SERPS).

Class 2 contributions

Class 2 contributions are a flat-rate amount, irrespective of your profits: the amount for the 1991–2 tax year is £5.15 a week. You can pay these contributions by buying a stamp every week at the post office and sticking it on a card the local DSS office will send you. Or you can pay by direct debit from your bank account. Use DSS form CF 11 in the back pocket of this Pack to make the arrangements.

You can claim exemption from paying Class 2 contributions if your net yearly earnings from self-employment are below a certain limit (£2,900 for 1991–2) – but you must apply for a certificate of exemption in advance.

NI 255: *Class 2 and 3 National Insurance Contributions – Direct Debit, the Easy Way to Pay*

NI 27A: *National Insurance for People with Small Earnings from Self-employment*

Class 4 contributions

These are payable by Class 2 payers whose taxable profits exceed a certain sum. For the 1991–2 tax year, Class 4 contributions are paid on taxable profits over £5,900 a year: the rate is 6.3 per cent of taxable profits between £5,900 and £20,280 a year.

Class 4 contributions are assessed and collected by the Inland Revenue along with the income tax on your profits. Half the amount of Class 4 contributions can be deducted from your taxable profits before working out the income tax bill.

NP 18: *Class 4 National Insurance Contributions*

SECTION

7 EMPLOYING PEOPLE

If working for yourself is successful, you may wish to bring in someone else to work for you. And with many types of business, you will have to employ people from the start.

The Department of Employment publishes some useful booklets on employment matters (listed below prefixed with the letters PL or DE). You can get these from any Employment Service office (addresses in the telephone book). The Advisory Conciliation and Arbitration Service also produces useful booklets on employer/employee relationships (listed below with the prefix ACAS).

RECRUITING STAFF

Before you begin to look for the right people, define exactly what their duties are to be and the experience, skills and qualities needed for the job. Consider whether you would prefer to recruit a full-time person or a part-time, casual or freelance worker. And think about how you will pay your staff: basic wages, piecework, commission, bonus and a share of the profits are all appropriate to different types of work.

You can find suitable applicants through the Employment Service Agency (which runs Jobcentres), local authority careers offices (run by local education authorities) or an employment agency (which will charge you a fee). You could advertise in newspapers (local, national or trade press), on local radio, by placing cards in local shops, or putting up a sign on your premises (check planning regulations). Or you could ask existing employees or other people you know for a recommendation.

If there are several applicants, send them details of your business, the job, the sort of person you need and the pay and conditions you are offering. Include a simple application form to fill in, or ask for a written letter of application. You will want details of education and training, experience and previous employers. Ask for at least two references, including one previous employer if possible – take these up either by telephone or in writing.

The best of the candidates should be shortlisted and interviewed. Prepare key questions to ask all those you interview, as this makes comparison easier. Try to let the interviewees do the talking. Ask about frequent changes in job, and probe complaints about previous employers – the answers may be revealing. Remember that the interview is a chance for you to sell your business, to attract the best employees.

Once you have made a decision, offer the job to the preferred candidate (see *Contract of employment*, below). If it is accepted, tell the other applicants and thank them for their interest.

ACAS 6: *Recruitment and Selection*

EQUAL OPPORTUNITIES

It is generally unlawful to discriminate on grounds of race or sex in employment. The law on sex discrimination also covers discrimination on grounds of being married (so that you can't specify that a job is done by a single woman, for example).

The legislation is comprehensive and includes the arrangements made for recruiting, training, promoting, disciplining, dismissing and retiring staff. It also covers indirect discrimination: setting conditions which are not justifiable and which affect one sex or racial group more than another (e.g. you employ people who must be able to lift heavy weights when this is not justifiable). There are limited exceptions where a person's sex or race is a genuine occupational qualification – working as a model, for example, or as a waiter in an Indian restaurant.

Among matters to bear in mind are:

- advertising jobs – always make it clear that applicants of any race, sex or marital status can apply
- selection of candidates – don't ask questions which imply that women aren't interested in a career, for example, or that members of ethnic minorities are unsuited for certain jobs
- provision of opportunities to staff – don't discriminate in who is given training, for example, or promoted
- pay and terms and conditions of employment – equal pay for like work, work rated as equivalent and work of equal value
- dismissals and disciplinary matters.

For more details, see *Equal Opportunities: a Guide for Employers* (Equal Opportunities Commission), *Equal Pay: a Guide to the Equal Pay Act* (PL 743) and *Employment: a Guide to the Race Relations Act* (from the Commission for Racial Equality). The EOC and CRE have both issued codes of practice for employers to cover equal opportunity employment practice on sex and race.

CONTRACT OF EMPLOYMENT

You enter into a contract of employment as soon as someone accepts a job which you have offered him or her. This contract is legally enforceable once that person starts work, so you should make the offer in writing, clearly stating the duties, terms and conditions. The job description you produced for applicants will normally form the basis of this – if you have agreed to vary what it says, be sure to spell this out.

By law, you must provide a written statement of terms and conditions for every employee who works for you full-time or part-time for more than 16 hours a week. This should be provided within 13 weeks of starting work, and could take the form of the job offer letter. It must include at least the following (solicitors can usually provide standard forms to set out these details):

- name of employer and employee
- date of starting employment
- whether employment with a previous employer counts as part of this employment (e.g. if you buy a business)
- title or description of employee's job
- rates of pay (including overtime if any) and how they are calculated
- whether payment is to be weekly, monthly, in arrears etc.
- hours of work (regular and overtime if applicable)
- holidays and holiday pay
- sick pay arrangements
- pension scheme arrangements (including whether there is a pension scheme contracted out of the State Earnings-Related Pensions Scheme)
- length of notice required from employer and employee
- grievance procedures and disciplinary rules (not necessary for small employers).

If any of these do not apply, the statement should say so. And the terms may not be altered in any way without the agreement of employer and employee. If you transfer or promote an employee, it may need a new written statement. Part-time workers who work more than eight hours a week and less than 16 hours are entitled to a similar statement after they have worked for you for five years.

Note that in addition to the terms and conditions of employment you agree with your employees, they have statutory rights to time off for trade union duties (within limits) and for public duties such as serving as magistrate or local councillor.

PL 700: *Written Statement of Main Terms and Conditions of Employment*

PL 702: *Time Off for Public Duties*

PL 871: *Union Membership and Non-membership Rights*

PL 716: *Individual Rights of Employees – a Guide for Employers*

Paying employees

With every wage payment, you must give each employee a wage slip showing gross pay, deductions (itemised to say what each is for) and net pay. Keep a copy of this for your own records, and also a wages book which can be used by Inland Revenue auditors to check that you have deducted the right amount of tax and National Insurance (see below). Your accountant will advise on this, or even look after the payroll for a fee.

In some trades and industries, there are legally enforceable minimum hourly pay and overtime rates for employees aged 21 and over. The rates are set by Wages Councils, covering industries such as retailing, catering, hairdressing and clothing manufacture. In these industries, it is a criminal offence to pay less than the appropriate minimum rates and there is a Wages Inspectorate to enforce the law.

Note that if you put employees on short time or lay them off with no pay or reduced pay, they may be entitled to a guarantee payment for up to five working days in any three months in which there is no work.

ACAS 2: *Introduction to Payment Systems*

PL 704: *Itemised Pay Statement*

PL 724: *Guarantee Payments*

Maternity rights

A woman employee expecting a child has the right to time off without loss of pay for antenatal care. If she is dismissed because she is pregnant or for reasons connected with pregnancy, this may qualify as unfair dismissal (see opposite).

A mother also has the right to return to work after a baby is born, provided certain conditions are met. For example, she must have worked for you for 16 or more hours a week for at least two years or eight to 16 hours a week for five years. She must keep working for you up to at least 11 weeks before the baby is due and return to work not later than 29 weeks after the birth. But if you have five or fewer employees at the time she starts her maternity leave, you may be able to argue that there is no suitable job for her to return to.

You don't have to pay maternity pay to a woman employee having a baby, but you may be responsible for paying a state benefit statutory maternity pay (SMP) when she stops work to have the baby. You can claim back any SMP you pay by deducting it from the National Insurance contributions you send off each month to the Inland Revenue.

PL 710: *Employment Rights for the Expectant Mother*

DSS booklet NI 257: *Employer's Guide to Statutory Maternity Pay*

Sick pay

If an employee is off for more than four working days, you may be responsible for paying a state benefit statutory sick pay (SSP) for up to 28 weeks of illness. The amount of SSP and the conditions for paying it are decided by the Government. You can claim back 80 per cent of the SSP you pay out by deducting it from the National Insurance contributions you send off each month to the Inland Revenue (small businesses may be able to reclaim more for longer illnesses).

DSS booklet NI 227: *Employer's Guide to Statutory Sick Pay*

Pensions

Unless you set up a contracted out pension scheme for your employees, they – and you – will pay National Insurance contributions at the higher rates for people who are not contracted out of the State Earnings-Related Pension Scheme (SERPS) – see page 18. However, while SERPS tops up the state basic pension in line with earnings during members' working life, it falls short in most cases of the benefits offered by a good employer's scheme. You should certainly encourage employees to take out a personal pension; for younger employees, it might also be worth their while to take out a personal pension in order to contract out of SERPS. If your business is successful, you could consider making contributions to employees' personal pension schemes, perhaps matching their contributions within limits (these contributions are an allowable expense of your business – see page 25).

PROBLEMS WITH EMPLOYEES

There is no law against dismissing an employee, so long as it is done in a way that is fair. However, a dismissed employee may bring a complaint of unfair dismissal to an industrial tribunal, which can order reinstatement or award compensation. An employee who resigns may claim 'constructive dismissal' where the employer has acted in such a way as to force the resignation. Defending a case at an industrial tribunal will cost you time and money, so it is important to adopt fair employment practices which avoid such complaints.

The first point to note is that it is generally much easier to dismiss someone when they first come to work for you. An employee can take you to an industrial tribunal only if he or she has been working for you 16 or more hours a week for more than two years or between eight and 16 hours a week for more than five years. But there is no qualifying period for employees who allege that they were dismissed on the grounds of race or sex discrimination, or because of trade union activity (either active membership of a union or refusal to join one).

If you do have to sack someone who may take you to an industrial tribunal, it is important to be able to demonstrate one of the following sufficient reasons for dismissal:

- misconduct at work
- inability to do the job
- redundancy – where you no longer need anyone to do the job
- statutory duties which mean that the employment cannot continue.

You should follow set procedures which give the employee the chance to save his or her job. This means adopting a fair procedure, exploring other options short of dismissal and giving the employee an opportunity to put his or her case. The existence and use of a disciplinary procedure with graded stages from informal counselling through verbal warnings to written warnings is part of this.

Very few dismissals come before industrial tribunals and fewer than two in five are upheld as unfair, so the difficulties are not so great. But ask your legal adviser to check your documents and procedures, and seek advice if you find that the parting of the ways is coming.

PL 707: *Rights to Notice and Reasons for Dismissal*

PL 714: *Fair and Unfair Dismissal: a Guide for Employers*

PL 715: *The Law on Unfair Dismissal: Guidance for Small Firms*

TAXING YOUR EMPLOYEES' EARNINGS

Employing people not only brings legal obligations, it also makes you a tax collector for the Government. You will be expected to deduct income tax from your employees' wages under the PAYE (Pay As You Earn) system. You will also have to deduct National Insurance contributions from their wages and pay employer's NI contributions on them.

As soon as you take on your first employee (even if only part-time), tell the tax office which deals with your business. They will tell you which tax office will deal with your PAYE matters, assign you a PAYE tax reference number and give you the name of a contact person to deal with queries. You will be sent a *New Employer's Starter Pack*, with the forms, tables and instructions you need to operate PAYE. This will include a copy of the *Employer's Guide to PAYE*, the handbook for operating the system.

Inland Revenue leaflet IR 53 *Thinking of Taking Someone On?* explains the procedure – copies from your local tax office or PAYE enquiry office (under *Inland Revenue – Taxes, HM Inspectors of* in the telephone book).

National Insurance

All employees have to pay Class 1 National Insurance contributions if their earnings are more than the lower earnings limit (£52 a week for the 1991–2 tax year), unless they are over state pension age (65 for men, 60 for women). If your business is a company, this also applies to your earnings as a director (though not to any dividends paid to you as a shareholder); if you are self-employed or in a partnership, you pay Class 2 and probably Class 4 contributions instead (see page 27). And where an employee pays Class 1 contributions, you will have to pay employer's contributions also, based on the employee's wages.

The rates of Class 1 National Insurance contributions are given in the Table. Some married women pay contributions at a special reduced rate of 3.85 per cent of their earnings over the lower earnings limit up to the upper earnings limit (in return for fewer benefits). And if you have set up a pension scheme for your employees which is contracted out of SERPS, the rates are somewhat lower – this is unlikely to concern you at this stage of your business. Note that while employees pay no contributions on earnings above a certain limit (the upper earnings limit – £390 a week for 1991–2), employer's contributions are paid on all earnings above the lower earnings limit.

DSS leaflet NP 15: *Employer's Guide to National Insurance Contributions*

Class 1 National Insurance contribution rates for 1991–2

Rates for contracted-in employees

Earnings per week	Weekly contributions employee	employer
Up to £52	nil	nil
£52–£84.99	£1.04 + 9% of earnings over £52	4.6% of earnings
£85–£129.99	£1.04 + 9% of earnings over £52	6.6% of earnings
£130–£184.99	£1.04 + 9% of earnings over £52	8.6% of earnings
£185–£390	£1.04 + 9% of earnings over £52	10.4% of earnings
Over £390	£31.04	10.4% of earnings

PAYE audit visits

From time to time, you may be visited by an auditor from the Inland Revenue to check that you are operating the PAYE system properly. He or she will look particularly carefully at payments to contractors and to part-timers such as cleaners (these must still be entered on your PAYE returns even if too low to pay tax). If you have been failing to operate PAYE properly, you will have to pay the tax owed – and for several years back as well. So make sure you stick to the rules: ask your accountant or PAYE tax office for advice.